Musical Instruments of East Africa

1 Kenya

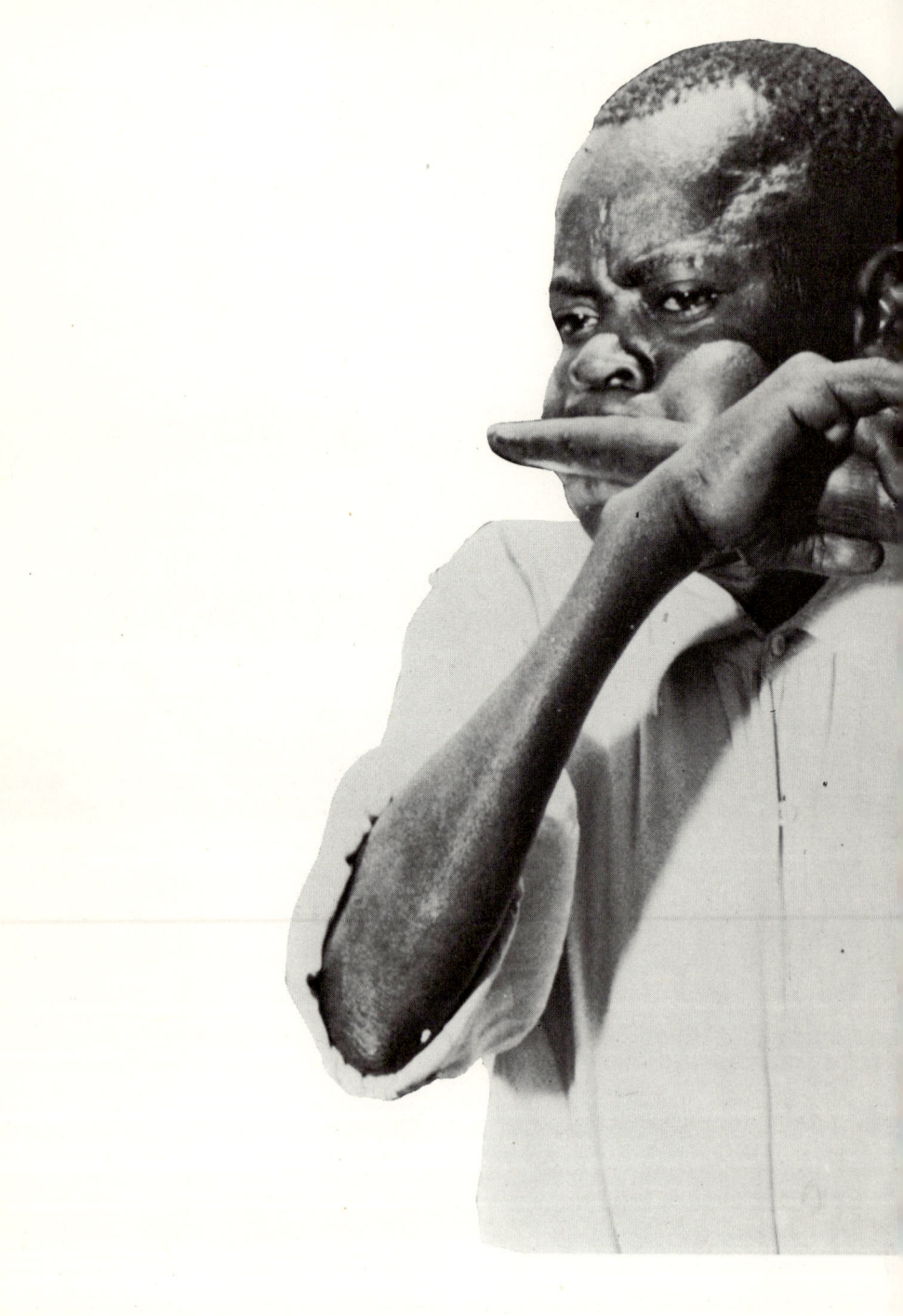

Notes by Graham Hyslop

Musical Instruments of East Africa

1 Kenya

Nelson

Nelson Africa Ltd
P.O. Box 73146 Nairobi

Thomas Nelson and Sons Ltd
36 Park Street London W1
77 Coffee Street San Fernando Trinidad

Thomas Nelson (Nigeria) Ltd
P.O. Box 336 Apapa Lagos

Thomas Nelson (Australia) Ltd
19-39 Jeffcott Street West Melbourne Victoria 3003

Thomas Nelson and Sons (Canada) Ltd
81 Curlew Drive Don Mills Ontario

© Graham Hyslop 1975

First published 1975

ISBN 0 17 511250 9

All rights reserved. No part of this publication
may be reproduced, stored in a retrieval system,
or transmitted, in any form or by any means,
electronic, mechanical, photocopying, recording or
otherwise, without the prior permission of the
publishers.

Phototypeset by Tradespools Ltd, Frome, Somerset
Printed by Butler and Tanner Ltd, Frome and London

Contents

vi	**List of illustrations**
vii	**Recordings** – Folk Music of East Africa 1. Kenya
1	**Preface**
3	**Foreword** – The Approach to this Study
5	**Instrumentalists and their Instruments**

Stringed Instruments

10	Ntono
14	Siiriri
17	Wandindi
18	Adeudeu
21	Litungu (Bukusu)
25	Litungu (Kuria)
28	Obukhana
31	Obokano

Wind Instruments

34	Oluika (Tachoni)
35	Oluika (Bukhayo)
37	Arupepe
38	Conch Shell
39	Mlele
40	Chivoti
42	Mwarutu
43	Bung'o or Nzumari

Percussion Instruments

46	Endonyi and Efumbu
48	Indonyi, Izidonyi and Ing'oma
50	Atenesu
52	Mutiiti and Isuguti
54	Kayamba
54	Mchirima, Chapuo and Gandu
62	**What of the Future?**
64	**Appendix**: Classification of Instruments

List of Illustrations

viii	Map

Stringed Instruments

8	Nyamuhanga with Ntono
10	Obokano, Obukhana and Ntono
15	Siiriri
16	Siiriri with Chisasi and Ikengere
18	Wandindi
18	Adeudeu
20	Longino Ebuu with Adeudeu
21	Litungu (Bukusu)
22	Litungu with Luhengere
25	Litungu (Kuria)
25	Bomwe with Litungu and Ibiturani bells
29	Makokha with Obukhana
33	Nyatama with Obokano

Wind Instruments

34	Oluika (Tachoni)
36	Oluika (Bukhayo)
38	Conch Shell
39	Isoka with Mlele
41	Chivoti and Kayamba
44	Juma Msafari with Nzumari – Bung'o

Percussion Instruments

47	Endonyi and Efumbu
49	Idonyi, Izidonyi and Ing'oma
51	Atenesu
55	Bumbumbu, Kayamba, Mchirima, Nzuga, Chigandu and Gandu
60/61	Group of coast musicians

Recordings

Folk Music of East Africa No. 1 (Kenya)
Philips (E.A.) label PKLP 102
P.O. Box 43695 Nairobi, Kenya

Side One
Stringed Instruments

Band 1 Ntono
Band 2 Siiriri with Chisasi and Ikengere
Band 3 Adeudeu
Band 4 Litungu (Bukusu)
Band 5 Litungu (Bukusu) with Luhengere
Band 6 Litungu (Kuria)
Band 7 Obokano

Side Two
Wind and Percussion

Band 1 Mwarutu and Kayamba
Band 2 Bung'o or Nzumari
Band 3 Indonyi, Izidonyi and Ing'oma
Band 4 Atenesu
Band 5 Mutiiti and Isuguti
Band 6 Mchirima, Chapuo and Chivoti
Band 7 Digo drums, Ukaya and Nzuga with Nzumari

Acknowledgements

The author and publishers are grateful to the Ministry of Information, Kenya for permission to reproduce the photographs and to *African Arts* for permission to reproduce material first published in *African Arts*, Vol. V, No. 4.

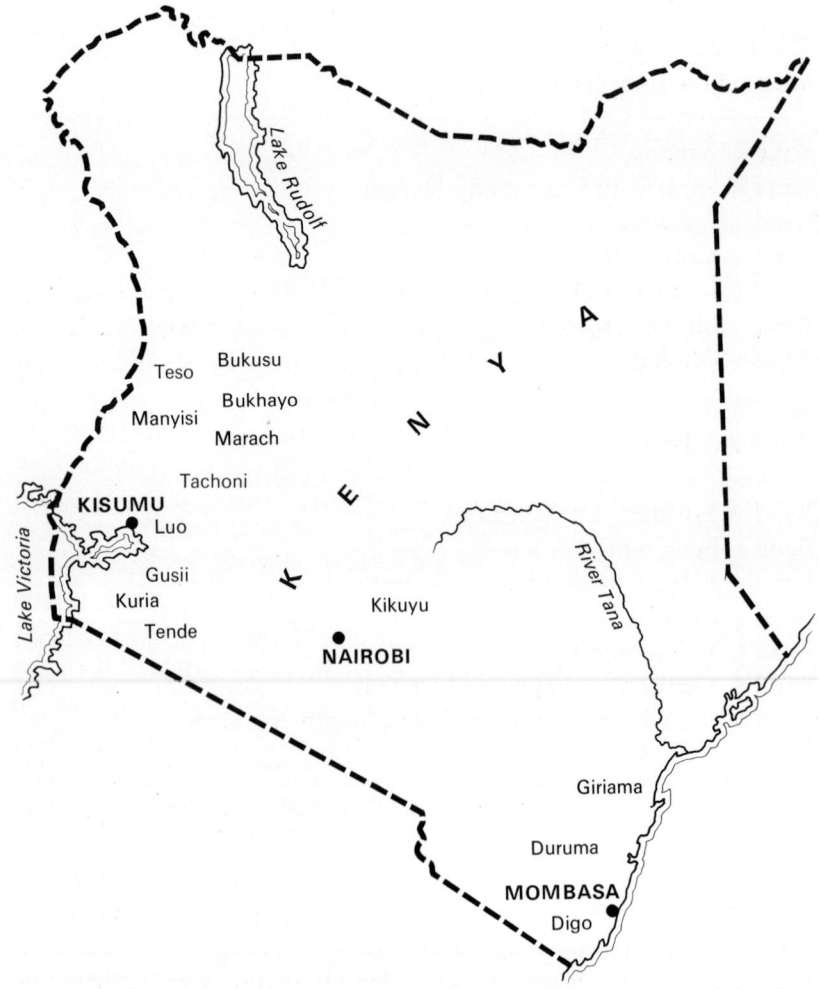

Map of Kenya showing approximately the areas in which the instruments mentioned in these *Notes* are found.

Preface

It is only natural that anyone interested in music of any part of the world, should have a particular interest in one branch or other of study. For myself, one of the aspects of African music which has captured my imagination is the study of traditional musical instruments. There are at least two reasons for this. In the first place, the infinite variety of instruments and their musical worth make the pursuit of knowledge about them intensely interesting in itself. Secondly, much can be learnt about the music generally of the area where such instruments are found, especially from the way in which they are tuned.

The instruments discussed here represent only a small proportion of the total number that are to be found in different parts of Kenya. They do represent however the main groups of stringed, wind and percussion instruments which make up such an important part of Kenya's rich musical heritage. On the other hand there must be many instruments hidden away in the rural areas about which practically nothing is yet known, outside the immediate district where they are made and played.

A word of explanation is needed as to the choice of instruments dealt with in these *Notes*. Those selected are the instruments I have had the opportunity to study fairly closely. In 1958 I was Music and Drama Officer for Kenya, and my work was based on the old Jeanes School at Kabete, near Nairobi where all kinds of resident courses were held in different fields of Adult Education. A colleague of mine, Mr Morris Mwendar, suggested that it would be a good idea to call together instrumentalists from as many parts of the country as possible so that a study might be made of their instruments. As nothing had been done at that time about this aspect of the music of Kenya, this seemed an excellent idea. Invitations were therefore sent out to all districts inviting instrumentalists to come together for some ten days, so that as much as possible could be learnt about their instruments – how they are made, how they are tuned and how they are played.

The response to this invitation varied considerably, and this was very largely due to the enthusiasm or otherwise of the Government Officers and others through whom the information was sent to the instrumentalists. At Bungoma near Mount Elgon, on the Kenya–Uganda border, the Secretary of the District Council supported the proposal whole-heartedly. He was most anxious that instrumentalists from his area should come to the Jeanes School, and in order that it would be possible to choose the best, a local Festival of traditional instruments was organised in which no less than ninety musicians took part. I was invited to adjudicate and chose the best fifteen. It was these who made up the greater part of the number who took part in the programme of study that year. The following year a similar course was organised and on that occasion there was a most welcome addition of a group of musicians from Kwale district at the coast, who brought with them some unusual and fascinating wind and percussion instruments.

The information given in these *Notes* is based on a study of the material collected on those two occasions. Much more work needs to be done however, to give a proper assessment of the whole picture concerning Kenya's musical instruments.

I should like to record my appreciation of the help given by Martin Mkombo in reading the script, and for his advice on matters of language and custom.

July, 1974   GRAHAM HYSLOP
University of Dar es Salaam
Tanzania

Foreword – The Approach to this Study

The method of approach to this study of some of the musical instruments of Kenya is naturally determined by the purpose it is meant to serve. While it is hoped that it will be of general interest to that ever widening circle of musicians who now take note of the music of Africa, it is intended mainly as a handbook for young musicians who are themselves *involved in* instrumental music-making in Africa.

In the first place this is an introduction to the instruments themselves, but it also gives an insight into the artistic integrity of the traditional instrumental music of Kenya, and this can help towards a greater appreciation of the skills of the instrumentalists as well. The instruments have been grouped in the conventional categories of strings, wind and percussion. It is necessary however for students to be aware of the terminology used in the Hornbostel–Sachs classification, and this information is given as an appendix.

There are more and more opportunities being offered for formal study of music in various parts of Africa, and the conventional language of music is becoming everywhere familiar. The aim of these *Notes* is to communicate as much information as possible in the most straightforward manner, and the approach is therefore as uncomplicated as can be. Staff notation has been used to indicate the tuning of the instruments, and for the transcription of instrumental music, songs and drum rhythms. Where the notation is uncertain in these terms, an indication is given by bracketing notes of doubtful pitch. It would have been possible to produce scientifically accurate mathematical tables showing the tuning of the instruments precisely in terms of vibrations per second, but such a method would most certainly have conveyed much less musically.

A word or two is necessary about the transcriptions themselves. It would be idle to claim one hundred per cent accuracy for these but in most cases they can be checked against the actual music, from the recordings listed on page vii. Most of the transcriptions were made long after the musicians had returned home, and they were therefore unavailable for further consultation. Difficulties arise in the transcription of the music of Kenya due to the fact that, generally speaking, the question of pitch does not seem to receive the same meticulous care that is given to matters of rhythm. Then again, concerning the tuning of instruments, stringed, wind or percussion, notes played one after the other are sometimes uncertain, and the pitch often has to be checked with the sounds produced during a performance. This is particularly true with stringed instruments when the traditional strings made of animal tendons are used, since the strength of the plucking of the string can be a factor in the clarity of note produced.

It is hoped that those young people now acquiring general musical knowledge will find ways of applying this to the development of traditional musical instruments and the music that is played on them. There are all kinds of possibilities, such as improvements in the construction of instruments and in the materials used, the widening of scope of performance, and the writing of new music firmly rooted in the old, both for solo and ensemble.

Instrumentalists and their Instruments

Professional instrumentalists in Kenya are almost exclusively men. Only once has there been mention of women instrumentalists. Two players of the *Atenesu* drum from Teso country at the foot of Mount Elgon said that they were taught by their mother, and one of these men was also teaching his daughter.

So far as the musicians mentioned in these *Notes* are concerned, whenever the question of the handing down of musical skills from one generation to another has been discussed, the information given has always shown that this is a strictly family affair. Never once has an instrumentalist said that he learnt to play his instrument from anyone outside the family circle, or that he was passing on his knowledge to anyone other than his own kith and kin. The commonest pattern that emerges is that any particular instrumentalist was taught by his father who in his turn received instruction from the grandfather. The player generally passes on his skill to his son. There are variations on this general theme, and it must be remembered that in African society the terms brother, father, uncle and so on do not necessarily convey the precise meaning indicated by the English names.

Instrumentalists have a recognised role in society and are often hired for particular functions, such as weddings, funerals or any kind of family or social celebration. They have the ability to adapt the words of any songs they sing to the occasion and will most certainly praise the person responsible for the invitation to play. Apart from any fee that will be paid, individuals quite frequently make small gifts of cash to show their appreciation of a performance. In the membrane of the resonating bowl of the Bukusu *Litungu* (see page 21) there is a hole just under $1\frac{1}{2}$ inches or 35 millimetres in diameter. When the player was asked what this was for he replied that it served the dual purpose of letting the sound out and the pennies in! This was obviously said in jest but it confirms this practice of giving small presents to an instrumentalist as he plays. Again on the top of the cross bar of the frame of the Kuria *Litungu* when it is held vertically in the playing position, there is a small tin lid fastened (see page 25). When this instrumentalist was asked a similar question about the use to which the tin was put he simply said, 'What am I to do with my cigarette ash?' This reply was clearly in the same spirit as that about the other *Litungu* and it is fairly obvious that the tin is in fact there to receive coins from admirers.

Instrumentalists in Kenya generally make their own instruments, although it is understood that amongst the Luo there are professional instrument makers. One of the musicians who came to the Jeanes School in 1958 was the late Maunda Waliaula, the finest player of the Bukusu *Litungu* heard so far. When he returned home he very generously presented the writer with his own instrument as a token of appreciation of the interest shown in his music-making. What this meant to him may be measured by the fact that he would have to go away and make another instrument. It was obvious that this particular instrument was fitted with commercial strings and it seemed that the very least that could be done for Waliaula was to provide him with a new set of strings. A visit was paid to a music shop in Nairobi and all kinds of manufactured strings were produced but none of them were the kind that this instrumentalist was looking for. The required strings were eventually obtained in a sports shop, as Waliaula had been in the habit of using nylon tennis racket gut. At the pitch required for this instrument, this material produced a very pleasant tone. The highest string incidentally was of wire.

This question of the use of manufactured strings for traditional instruments in Kenya sometimes raises issues of musical importance. Originally strings were made from twisted leg tendons of cattle and other similar material. It is a rather tiresome business to obtain such material and treat it properly and as ready-made strings of one kind or another become available, it is only natural that musicians should want to make use of them. Another instrumentalist who came to the Jeanes School in 1958 was Jones Bomwe with his Kuria *Litungu* and at that time he was using traditional strings which gave the instrument a pitch well down in the bass range. In 1963, five years later, he was invited to play at a special concert in the Kenya National Theatre in connection with Independence celebrations. In the years between, Bomwe had changed over to manufactured strings and the musical effect was quite dramatic and just a little disturbing. The new strings were finer than those used originally and had the effect of forcing the pitch of the instrument very much higher than it had been before. The shock on hearing the instrument on this second occasion was very much the same as that which one would experience when meeting an old friend whom one had known to have a deep bass voice, only to discover that he had changed to an alto!

This is the point at which the question has to be asked as to whether it is a good thing to change to manufactured materials in the construction of musical instruments, when so doing changes their whole character. The trouble in this particular case is that commercial strings which can produce a note of low enough pitch to correspond to the original strings are difficult to obtain in rural areas in Africa and they are very expensive. In 1968 an experiment was being made at the Institute of Ethnomusicology at the University of California in Los Angeles with the use of different thicknesses of nylon fishing line for stringed musical instruments. This kind of thing may prove a possible solution to the problem in Kenya of finding inexpensive strings of sufficient thickness to produce notes of low pitch so that the original character of an instrument is maintained.

The introduction of modern materials in the construction of traditional instruments is very often the result of looking for time and labour saving techniques. A good example is the making of the *Atenesu* drums from Teso country. The illustration of two of these drums on page 51 shows quite clearly that they were made from an empty four-gallon square petrol can, known locally as a debi, and a discarded bucket. The resultant tone is harsh and inferior to that produced on a drum with a wooden base. A mellow toned drum is not always required and the two small *Endonyi* drums played with the *Efumbu* in Bukusu country (see page 47) give a bright sharp tone. Even in this case however the softer toned *Efumbu* tends to be muffled by the two *Endonyi* when they are played together.

Another percussion instrument with which experiments have been made with modern materials is the *Kayamba* (see page 55). This is normally made from two layers of reeds with hard seeds in between. Once – and fortunately only once – a pair of *Kayamba* was seen made from two sides of a petrol can with something like ball bearings inside. This definitely ruined the whole character of this instrument and it sounded much more like a train rattling over railway lines than a musical instrument.

Nyamuhanga Kyaro with *Ntono*

Stringed Instruments

From the number of very interesting stringed instruments that have already come to light in Kenya, it would appear that there is a greater variety of this kind of instrument than of any other category. They are found more particularly around the shores of Lake Victoria and in Western Kenya generally, but also in smaller numbers elsewhere.

From time to time there has been considerable argument about the origin of stringed instruments. Professor Kirby, writing about the musical instruments of Southern Africa,[1] says of the stringed instruments that these 'would appear to have originated, directly or indirectly, from the bow of the hunter, and it is interesting to find in this country clear evidence of such development at different stages.' Kirby quotes Henry Balfour as saying over seventy years ago that 'writers of all ages have drawn attention to the musical note emitted by the bow-string when released in shooting, and dwell upon the delight which it affords to the archer's ear.'[2] It certainly seems reasonable that this might lead the hunter himself, or someone else who was musical, to develop the use of the bow as a musical instrument.

In an article by Dr Wachsmann who was once Curator of the Kampala Museum in Uganda, written in 1961,[3] it is pointed out that twenty years after Balfour, a Swiss anthropologist named Montandon took the view that the hunter's bow derived *from* the musical bow! Another authority on musical instruments, Curt Sachs, however, denies that there is any connection between the musical bow and that of the hunter. He says that the idea is 'plausible, but wrong, like many plausible explanations.'[4]

---

[1] Kirby, Percival R., *The Musical Instruments of the Native Races of South Africa*, Oxford 1934, Johannesburg 1953.
[2] Balfour, Henry, *The Natural History of the Musical Bow*, Oxford 1899.
[3] Wachsmann, K. P., *Musical Instruments through the Ages*, Edited Anthony Baines, London London 1961.
[4] Sachs, Curt., *The History of Musical Instruments*, London 1942.

Left – *Obokano*, Kisii; Right – *Obukhana*, Marach; Centre – *Ntono*, with *Kiti* (Striker), *Enkoo* (Finger stall) and *Mbirii* (Bell), Watende; Lower Centre – *Tindeche* (Ankle bells) and *Esidiri* (Toe ring) used with *Obukhana*, Marach; Lower Right – Head-dress worn by player of *Obukhana*.

Ntono

It is certain that the *Ntono* which is found amongst the Watende on the Kenya–Tanzania border, gives the impression of having derived directly from the hunter's bow. Nowadays it has refinements over a simple hunting weapon which have developed with its use as a musical instrument, but this cannot be taken as evidence against its having developed originally from the hunter's bow.

The *Ntono* has a wire string that runs from one end of the bow to the other. It is caught at a point which produces the following notes on the shorter and longer sections of the string.

Transposed down a semitone

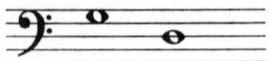

The interval between these two notes is interesting. In tonic sol-fa it is d^1–s. In staff notation it is known as a perfect fourth. This is a basic feature of musical tonality and a natural interval that belongs just as much to physics as it does to music.

At the point where the string is caught, there is a resonating gourd fastened to the bow and held against the player's body. The instrument is held in the left hand just above the gourd. On the middle finger of the left hand, the player wears a kind of finger-stall which it is understood is made from the neck of the gourd. When this is pressed against the upper and longer section of the bow string, a third note is produced. The interval between this note and that on the open longer section of the string is some kind of second above it, but it is difficult to define accurately.

The *Ntono* is played by striking the wire with a fine stick known as *kiti* which is held in the player's right hand. A delightful gentle percussion accompaniment is provided by a small pea-pod shaped bell called *mbirii*, worn on the little finger of the right hand. Some 10 cm from the top of the bow, the string is caught again and it is understood that this provides an adjustment for fine tuning.

Stringed instruments in Kenya are generally regarded as serving the purpose of providing an accompaniment to a song which the player himself sings. In many cases this accompaniment is made up of a repetitive phrase of two, four or eight bars, over which the singer supplies his own much more elaborate and varied melody. This kind of accompaniment is not unlike the *Ground bass* which Scholes has described as 'a short bass phrase repeated many times with varied upper parts.'[1] The interest of the melody above the bass can completely disguise the simplicity of the accompaniment. It is to be hoped that stringed instruments in Kenya will sometime be liberated from their present rather subservient role of a mere accompaniment, and will be recognised as a source of instrumental music in its own right.

Here is the two bar phrase which makes up the instrumental accompaniment on the *Ntono* for one song.

Transposed down a semitone

[1] Scholes, Percy A., *The Concise Oxford Dictionary of Music*, London 1952.

At the beginning of this song the instrumental phrase is repeated a few times and at the end of the fourth entry, the singer begins to sing. The vocal entry always comes somewhere in the bar marked *. Five times at the beginning this happens on the last quaver of the bar, but at the next entry, it is on the third quaver. As the song develops, the gap between the vocal phrases closes and sometimes there is only a semi-quaver rest between them, but always there is some break, however short, at the beginning of bar *. It will be seen that the phrases of the accompaniment and the vocalist overlap.

Precision in the transcription of the vocal parts is difficult, particularly with regard to the semi-quavers. This is partly due to the occasional use of glissando, the technique of sliding from one note to another. The vocal part written on the double G clef sounds an octave below that which is written.

There are certain dissonances between the instrumental and vocal parts. In the first vocal phrase there is a C sounding above a D and an A only a major second above a G. These would be noticed by few in a performance, due to some extent to the independent semi-quaver movement of the voice and instrument. There is frequently however a simple octave on the strong beat after bar *, and more often than not, the vocal phrase ends on a note which is consonant with the instrument. Sometimes the vocal phrase ends on an A, giving the impression of an intermediate cadence.

It is interesting to note that the tonal centre or 'home note' of the vocal line and the instrumental accompaniment are not the same. The music of the *Ntono* is centred on D, but the voice part frequently, and certainly finally, comes to rest firmly on G. It is as if the two parts were using two different 'scales' whose tonal centres are a perfect fourth part.

Here is a transcription of the end of the song.

The dotted quaver in the final bar makes up for what was missing in the opening bar of the instrumental accompaniment.

Siiriri

The *Siiriri* is an example of a kind of instrument, with either one or two strings, that is to be found all over Africa. Even within Kenya itself there are several names by which this instrument is known. The Luo variety, which has one string, is called *Orutu*. The Kikuyu version, known as *Wandindi*, has two strings, so has the *Ishiriri*, one of the varieties found in Western Kenya.

The *Siiriri* comes from Bukusu country. It has two strings, tuned like the *Ntono* to a perfect fourth, but at a higher pitch.

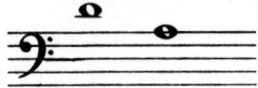

The base of the *Siiriri* is a small resonating drum. Hide is stretched across the top but the other end is left open. The stem or 'neck' of the instrument is a stick penetrating right through the drum, just under the membrane, and protruding a little on the further side. The strings, which in this particular instrument were made of wire, are fastened near the top of the neck with a wooden peg, or sometimes a nail. They run down the neck and across the drum which acts as a soundboard, being supported by a small bridge made from a small section of fine bamboo. The strings are finally secured to the end of the stem protruding from the drum.

The *Siiriri* is played with a small bow, the strings of which are made from sisal. All string players who use a bow need resin of some kind to rub on the bow strings to ensure that they grip firmly and produce good clean tone. With this instrument, local resin obtained from a certain tree is used. In order that it is ready to hand for use, a small lump is fixed to the side of the drum, just under the stem.

It is clear from any performance on the *Siiriri* that the second (lower) string is quite certainly a fairly recent addition. One player thought this innovation was introduced around 1939. Very limited use is made of it, chiefly as a drone with an additional note at each cadence.

As with the *Ntono*, the *Siiriri* supplies an accompaniment to a song made up of a repetitive phrase, in this case of four bars. The main tune of the accompaniment played on the D string has many variations but the use of the A string is restricted to a rhythmic drone on the open string with a middle C added at the end of each phrase. This often

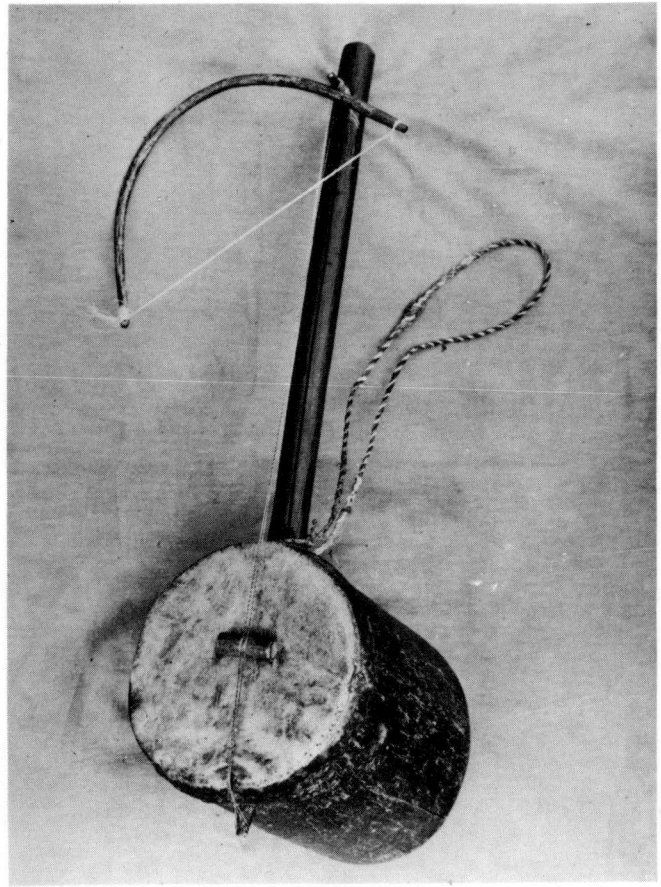

Siiriri (Bukusu)

produces a discord against the open D string and a D in the voice part too. At the beginning of one song there is a distinct discord involving something like a G♯ against this open A string. This may or may not be deliberate.

Apart from this initial G♯, only five notes are heard on the D string:

The voice range covers a major sixth. As is frequent in African vocal music, there is considerable slurring between the various intervals.

Siiriri with *Chisasi* and *Ikengere*

The *Siiriri* is sometimes accompanied by two simple percussion instruments, neither of which is traditional or very musical. One is the *Chisasi* which is simply an empty tin filled with bicycle ball bearings. These are played in pairs, one tin held in each hand. This is obviously a rather poor imitation of the traditional gourd filled with hard seeds or small stones. The other instrument is the *Ikengere*, which is just a piece of steel, bent into a semi-circle, and struck with another piece of metal, rather like a coarse *triangle*. The idea of introducing this kind of percussion sound is good, and no doubt the *Ikengere* will be refined to play a more musical part in such an ensemble. The rhythm of these two percussion instruments is constant.

The rhythm of the *Siiriri* is typically complex, indicating at times a clear duple beat against the triple.

Wandindi

Two examples of the *Wandindi* can be seen overleaf. One has two strings tuned in one of two ways, either

    a perfect fourth apart   or   a perfect fifth

The first tuning is almost identical to the *Siiriri*, being the same interval and only a semitone higher.

The second *Wandindi* only has one string and when played together with the two stringed instrument, is tuned to match the upper note.

There are differences in the construction of the *Wandindi* from that of the *Siiriri*. In the first place, the base of the resonating drum in this case is a tin, instead of being carved out of wood. Both ends of the drum are covered with hide, with a hole on the underside to release the sound. It is said that the original tuning pegs of the *Wandindi* were similar to those of the *Siiriri* but the present system has been adapted from the guitar. The strings used on the instruments illustrated were also those of the guitar. The overall length of the instrument is some 70 cm ($27\frac{1}{2}$ ins) and the diameter of the drum about 13 cm (5 ins).

The Wandindi is sometimes accompanied by a small percussion instrument known as the *Gichandi*, which is made out of a gourd and filled with small smooth stones to make a rattle.

Njoroge Kamau and Joseph Kamau with two *Wandindi* and Mbote Kahuko who plays the *Gichandi*

Wandindi

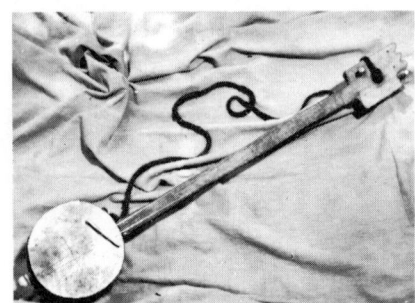

Adeudeu

The *Adeudeu* is a beautifully made five stringed harp from Teso country in Elgon district. The base is an oblong resonating bowl, made of wood completely covered with hide. There is a hole in the membrane

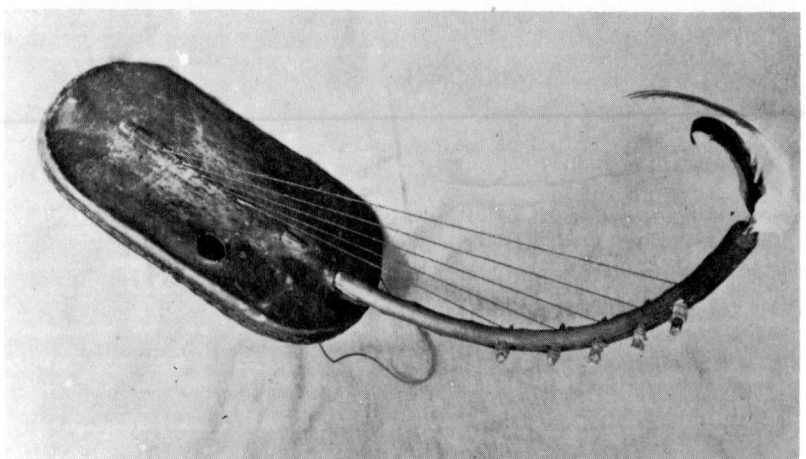

Adeudeu (Teso)

on the top of the bowl which is obviously meant to release the sound. The stem of the instrument runs part of the way under the membrane and then extends outwards and upwards in a curve. It is on the curve that the tuning pegs are fixed, about 5 cm (2 ins) apart. On the instrument studied there was an extra peg hole at the top of the stem which was not used. The strings are fastened at one end to that part of the stem which is under the membrane of the bowl and are then stretched diagonally across the instrument to the tuning pegs. The strings on the instrument illustrated here are of traditional material, made from twisted tendons. They give a soft, almost a muffled tone which makes it difficult to be certain of precise pitch. There is a touch of festivity with the feathers which decorate the top of the stem.

This is the tuning of the five strings, transposed up a semitone.

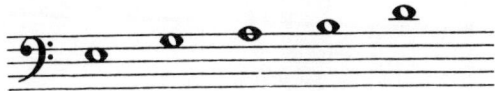

There is considerably more variety in the music produced on the *Adeudeu* than on either the *Ntono* or the *Siiriri*. In the first place instead of their being continuous singing, there are alternate instrumental and vocal sections. The themes are varied and the phrases are of different lengths. An analysis of one song and its accompaniment will illustrate these features. In one performance the instrumental introduction contained a variety of musical ideas and the rhythm was in a fairly free style, something in the nature of a recitative. At the entry of the voice part a much firmer rhythm was established in compound triple time. At this point the accompaniment is modified, a percussion figure being added by the player tapping out a rhythm on the drum like top of the bowl. Both the vocal part and the instrumental interludes are of unequal length varying generally between five and eight bars, although one vocal section was of some twelve bars.

Here is the opening of the instrumental introduction.

Longino Ebuu and *Adeudeu*

This is an example of the kind of instrumental interlude that occurs between the vocal sections.

Typically, there is a counter rhythm produced by plucking the E string twice against the three main beats of the bar.

The vocal sections differ each time because of the words. It may well be that there is an element of spontaneity in the choice of words and this would certainly account for the difference in rhythm and length of phrases. The general shape of the melody however is constant, always beginning with a reciting note on high E and ending with the cadence on A. The following is a sketch of one of the vocal sections.

It will be seen that as in the case of the *Ntono*, the final note of the voice part is a perfect fourth above that of the instrument.

Litungu (Bukusu and Tachoni)

The *Litungu* is a seven stringed instrument from Bukusu country and also from Tachoni. The instrument illustrated below is from Bukusu. The overall length is about 90 cm (3 ft). The resonating wooden bowl is

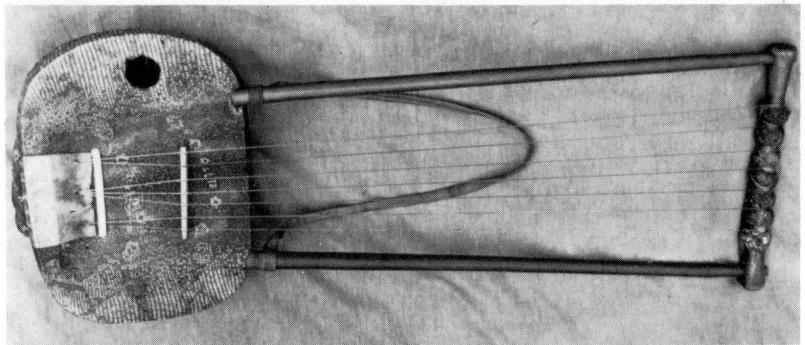

Litungu (Bukusu)

33.5 cm by 25 cm and 15 cm deep (13 ins × 10 ins × 6 ins). A wooden frame juts out of the bowl and measures approximately 65 cm in length and 30 cm across the top (26 ins × 12 ins).

The bowl is carved out of a solid block of wood and is covered on the top with membrane, in this particular case, giant lizard skin. The strings run from the cross bar at the top of the frame, down the length of the instrument and across the membrane, being supported by a small fretted wooden *bridge*. The strings are held in position on the cross bar by knobbles of string wound round and round. These knobbles act as a tuning device, a system used on other stringed instruments in Kenya. Below the bridge, the strings are taken through the membrane into the bowl and out again through the wooden base of the instrument where they are anchored to a small metal rod. Just below the bridge the strings are divided into three groups, two together on either side, and three in the middle. The strings used in the instrument studied were of nylon tennis racket gut, with the exception of that for the highest note which was of wire.

When played, the *Litungu* is held in one of two positions, either straight up in front of the player, or across the lap. The player normally sits. This instrument is often played in pairs and as with other stringed instruments, there is a song, sung by one of the players, but with the

Three *Litungu* (Bukusu) with *Luhengere*

second player joining in from time to time. The chief instrumentalist introduces himself and his song in plain speech against an instrumental accompaniment, and there is a return to plain speech occasionally during a performance.

Two percussion instruments are sometimes used with the *Litungu*. These are the *Luhengere* and the common ankle bells. The *Luhengere* is made of wood, in the form of a long narrow arch, and is struck with sticks, two in each hand. The *Luhengere* and the ankle bells have not been heard played together with the *Litungu*, it has always been one or the other. The added percussion accompaniment invariably introduces a contrast in rhythm with the strings, sometimes three against four, or two against three.

There are two patterns of tuning and each of them suggests a different pattern of tonality. One, which probably reflects the traditional style is as follows (left to right):

Transposed down a semitone

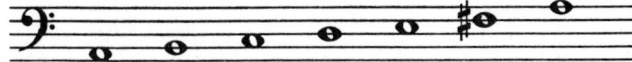

At least two systems of tonality are used with this tuning. The first is a major mode based on the C with a pattern in the bass like this.

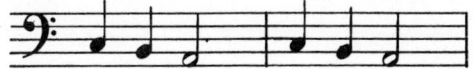

This shows only the lowest notes in the accompaniment. There is an intricate pattern of notes on the other strings. The voice enters on a high C. At the end of the song, the final cadence in the vocal part falls to the G, above a C in the instrumental accompaniment.

Voice

Litungu

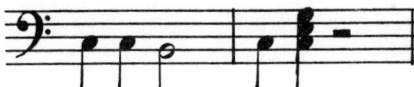

Another centre of modality used with this tuning is a minor mode based on B. The soloist enters on a high F♯ falling to the tonic B. The voice part clings to this B as a kind of reciting note. In the accompaniment there is continual alternation between the B minor chord and the A minor chord a full tone below. The final note in the voice part is again B. However in the accompaniment there is an unexpected cadence leading to D major, with the bass rising from the A.

The second method of tuning has a major third from the lowest note:

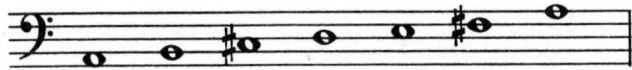

This tuning definitely introduces a tonic-dominant kind of harmony, very much like the chords used by amateurs on the guitar. Here is the opening of a song, again of course with decorations on the other strings.

The voice part follows an exactly similar tonal pattern in a firmly established major key, centred on D.

Litungu (Kuria)

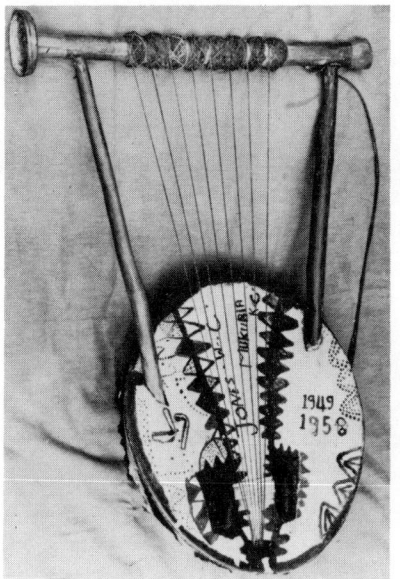

Litungu (Kuria)

Bomwe with *Litungu* (Kuria) and *Ibiturani* bells

It is interesting to note that people as far apart as Mount Elgon on the Kenya-Uganda border, and Gisii on the Tanzania border both call one of their stringed instruments by the same name – *Litungu*. The Elgon version is found in Bukusu and Tachoni country and that of Kisii in the Kuria area. Although the name is the same, the two instruments are quite different, in construction, the number of strings, method of tuning and the way they are played.

The Kuria *Litungu* has a large resonating bowl, some 42 cm (16½ ins) in diameter. This would traditionally have been carved out of a large block of wood but on the instrument studied an iron *karai* was used, a large metal basin used for carrying loads or bathing the baby – to mention only two of its many uses. The question of making use of ready-made materials in the construction of traditional instruments has already been discussed but in this particular case the tone of the instrument does not seem to have suffered from the substitution of metal for wood. It would be interesting to compare two instruments, one with a metal and the other with a wooden resonating bowl. The *karai* in this particular instrument was completely covered with zebra skin, disguising its homely appearance.

A sturdy wooden frame juts out of the bowl, 42 cm (16½ ins) long, and widening to 60 cm (2 ft) across the top. Like its Bukusu namesake, the strings of the Kuria *Litungu* are fastened by means of knobbles onto the cross bar. They run the length of the instrument across a *bridge* resting on the membrane of the bowl. The *bridge* in this case is made from strips of wood held in position by lumps of bees' wax.

The *Litungu* is accompanied by a percussion instrument which consists of three large pea-pod shaped bells, known as *Ibiturani*. They are tied with leather thongs onto the end of a long stick which is held between the player's big toe and the one next to it. This stick is struck against the lower frame of the instrument, and provides a sturdy bell accompaniment.

The player of the instrument studied was Jones Bomwe and one of his names was painted on the top of the resonating bowl amongst gay decorations. The date 1949 indicates the year in which the instrument was made. Bomwe was taught by his father and intended to teach his son. His grandfather also played the *Litungu*, illustrating the tradition of passing on musical skills from one generation to the next.

The Kuria *Litungu* has eight strings tuned as follows:

The pattern of the order of notes in this system of tuning is the same for all instruments of this type studied so far in Kenya. Unlike the Bukusu *Litungu* in which the octave is found between the first and the last strings, here the octave comes between the two middle strings, the fourth and the fifth. This may seem strange but so is the order of letters on the keyboard of a typewriter! Someone, at some time, decided that this is the best arrangement of letters for making words. Similarly, this system of tuning has evolved as the best arrangement on this kind of instrument for making music. One other point to notice about the tuning of this *Litungu* is that the first two notes are repeated on the last two strings.

The music played on this instrument is of the same pattern as that found on other stringed instruments. There is a repetitive phrase which serves as an accompaniment to a song, sung by the instrumentalist.

In one song, the percussion accompaniment on the bells produces a most unusual rhythmic complexity. Heard alone, the stringed accompaniment sounds like this:

This produces a grouping of 8 quavers divided into 3 + 3 + 2. When the bell accompaniment is introduced however, the effect is as follows:

Here the arrangement of quavers fits into a simple quadruple time with a crochet beat.

The voice part occurs in regular short phrases. The range is within the octave from Middle C to an octave above (actual pitch B). The phrases are in pairs, one generally starting on high C and finishing on Middle C, the other beginning on G and ending with a cadence on D, which slips onto Middle C, in the style of an *appoggiatura*.

The shape of the vocal part is shown below with the stringed instrument and the bells.

In another song there is a combination of rhythms involving two against three between the *Litungu* and the bells.

In this performance the E string sounds much more like an F and is transcribed as such below.

Obukhana

In the Elgon area there is another eight stringed instrument constructed in very much the same way as the Kuria *Litungu*. It is called *Obukhana* and is found among the Marach people. In the instrument studied the overall length was 65 cm ($25\frac{1}{2}$ ins), and the wooden resonating bowl, made from the *Omukhuyu* tree measured 33 cm × 26.5 cm × 16.5 cm deep (13 ins × $10\frac{1}{2}$ ins × $6\frac{1}{2}$ ins). The side struts of the main frame were made from the *Olukhuma* and the wood of the cross bar which measured 38 cm (15 ins) was that of the *Oluweyiwe*.

There is a photograph on page 10 showing the front of the instrument. It will be seen that the strings run the length of the instrument in the same way as in the Kuria *Litungu* crossing a little *bridge* on the membrane, in this case constructed from two strips of bamboo and one of wood, held in position as before by bees' wax – *Yuula*. In the forefront of the picture can be seen two percussion aids. There is a bunch of ankle bells called *Tindeche* and a metal toe ring (attached to

Makokha Owori with *Obukhana*

a cord) which the player wears on the big toe of his right foot. In the lower right-hand corner can be seen the head-dress sometimes worn by the instrumentalist, Makokha.

In the photograph on page 29 a small trap door can be seen in the back of the wooden bowl and this enables the player to store his percussion aids inside the instrument.

Here is the tuning of the eight strings.

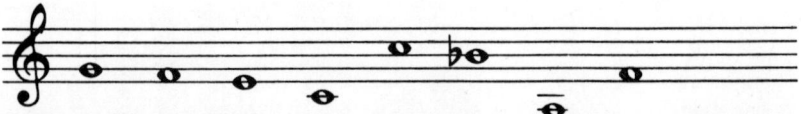

The seventh note in this series is interesting. In the tuning of the Kuria *Litungu*, the notes of each half of the strings ran roughly parallel to one another. This is so with the *Obukhana* with the exception of this one note which seems to have slipped an octave. If the A were on the treble clef, the same parallelism would be found as before. This tuning may be a personal preference of this particular instrumentalist, rather than a regular feature of the *Obukhana*. Washington Omondi has found similar variations in the tuning of the Luo lyre.

Here is the instrumental introduction to one song.

The two bars marked 'a' form the basis of the repetitive phrase common in stringed instruments as the accompaniment to a song. As in the case of the Bukusu *Litungu*, there is a spoken introduction against an instrumental accompaniment and the player reverts to plain speech again during the performance. Here is the beginning of the vocal part. The percussion bells and metal ring continue as before.

The vocal phrases vary in length and they begin on different notes, B flat, A, G, F or D. They generally end on F and (rarely) D. In the performance recorded, the tempo increased to 136 crotchets per minute, particularly near the end of the song. There is new musical material in the instrumental part as the song draws to a close.

Obokano

It was noticed that there was one instrument called *Litungu* in Mount Elgon district, and another of the same name in Gisii. Similarly there is an instrument in Gisii called *Obokano* a name very much like the *Obukhana* from Elgon.

The Kisii *Obokano* is the largest stringed instrument seen by this writer anywhere in Africa. It could be called the *Double Bass* of Kenya. The overall length of the instrument studied was 1 metre 6 cm (42 ins) and the resonating bowl was 45.5 cm long, 43 cm wide and 23 cm deep. (18 ins × 17 ins × 9 ins.) The cross bar measured 78 cm (31 ins).

There is a photograph of the *Obokano* on page 10 and the contrast in size with its near namesake the *Obukhana* is very clear. The *bridge* is naturally larger than on any other instrument as are the enormous lumps of bees' wax which hold the strips of cane (or some such material) in place.

There is no percussion instrument used with the *Obokano*.

The strings on this particular instrument were made from traditional material, leg tendons of cattle, and they were tuned as follows, and as with the Double Bass they reach well down below the range of the human voice.

The nature of the strings and the low pitch at which they were tuned made precision of pitch difficult to define. To give one example, the player plucked the strings one after the other, first in one direction and then in the other. The third note sounded E when played in one direction, but clearly as an E flat in the reverse order.

There are several points of particular interest in the vocal part in one performance heard on the *Obokano*.

In the first place, unlike the more recitative style employed with other stringed instruments, the words fitted the tune in a strictly rhythmic fashion and the whole melody was repeated several times with apparently very few minor variations.

The grouping of the phrases was also unusual. The simplest way to describe this is to regard the arrangement as being that of four sets of five bars shown by the square brackets. In three cases there are two phrases of two bars with a bar's rest, but in the second set there is one phrase of two bars and another of three.

Nyatama Onchuru with *Obokano*

Wind Instruments

If the first stringed instrument was possibly the hunting bow, it certainly seems probable that the first wind instrument to be used by man could have been the horn. Horns would be readily available, either after an animal had been slaughtered, or on the skeleton of a wild beast in the bush. Man's curiosity would prompt him to experiment and eventually he would find that by blowing into a horn a note or two could be produced.

There are many wind instruments made from horns to be found in Kenya and other parts of Africa and they differ in construction, in the way they are played, and in the vocal accompaniment that goes with them.

Oluika (Tachoni)

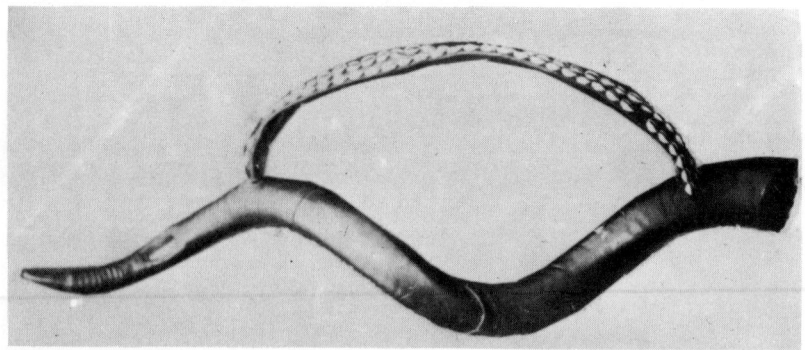

Oluika (Tachoni)

There is the *Oluika* from Tachoni country in Elgon. The particular horn illustrated here was very old, having belonged to the great-grandfather of the man who was playing it in 1958. It had skipped a generation as this player had been taught by his grandfather. It is the horn of an animal known locally as the *semberere*. It is side blown, the mouthpiece being cut in the side of the instrument near the narrower end. This is true of all horns so far found in Kenya. There was a strap attached to the instrument for carrying it. This was decorated with cowrie shells and this is another indication of the age of the instrument as such shells are seldom used nowadays for such purposes.

Musically this horn plays a very simple role, basically just supplying a drone on the note E above middle C as an accompaniment to a song. With stringed instruments it is the minstrel himself who sings. With wind instruments this is obviously impossible, so a friend is called in to assist. Below is given a sketch of one song with the *Oluika*. The four bars are repeated over and over again.

In 1958, the player of this horn, Daudi Wakame, was teaching his eleven year old son, but using a smaller horn, as the young boy would probably not have enough breath to blow the long instrument played by his father.

Oluika (Bukhayo)

There is another horn called *Oluika* found in the neighbouring district of Bukhayo, This instrument is in fact made from two horns joined together, the joint being wrapped round with hide. The sharper end is the horn of an animal called *Ikhulu*, a species of buck. The wider part is the stub of a homely cattle horn. The reason why this instrument was made in this way in the first instance was no doubt due to the fact that the player could not find a single horn that would produce either the pitch or tone required.

The player never seems to stop to take a breath, but the solution to this problem may be found in the regular 'scooped' notes rising to an

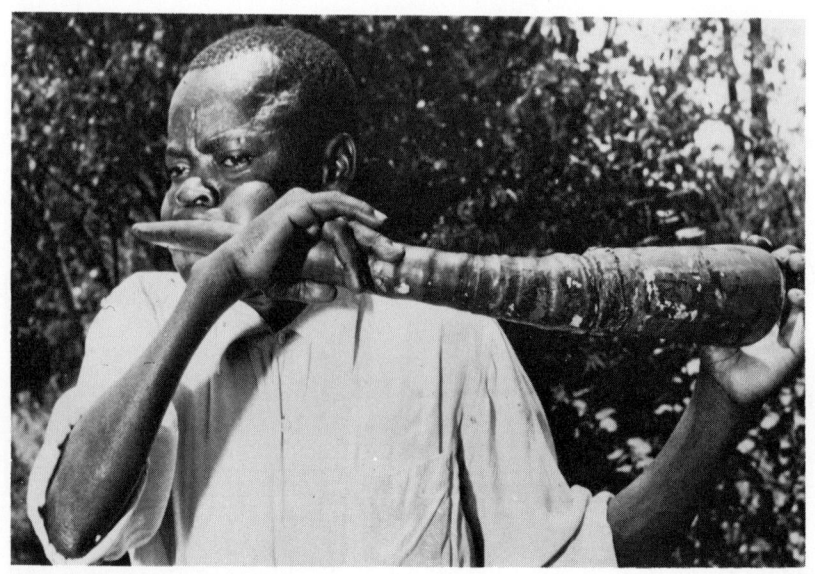

Kwerekho with *Oluika* (Bukhayo)

uncertain seventh above the fundamental note. These may be produced by a quick intake of breath.

There is more musical interest in the way this Bukhayo *Oluika* is played than with its Tachoni counterpart. There is a firmer rhythmic foundation which is strengthened by a percussion accompaniment supplied by ankle bells worn by the player. The vocalist in one performance was Lori. Here is a transcription of a song and its accompaniment.

The horn illustrated opposite measures some 64 cm (25 ins) in length and the unevenly shaped open end was 8 cm (3¼ ins) at its widest point. The mouthpiece cut into the side of the horn, as with the Tachoni instrument, is 4 cm (1½ ins) long. A hole drilled through the tip at the sharp end is doubtless intended for a cord by which the horn could be carried.

With the Bukusu *Litungu*, the instrumentalist introduced a song in plain speech against an instrumental accompaniment. With the Bukhayo *Oluika*, the singer concludes the song by speaking in his ordinary voice. It will be seen in the transcription that in bar 3 there is a pause in the vocal part. It is at this point just before the end of the song that the vocalist introduces plain speech. He then returns once more to his singing as in bars 1 and 2. At bar 3 the last time he again speaks and continues to do so with the return to bar 1, at which point the song ends.

The player of this horn was a competent and experienced player. Over the years he had played with such energy that when blowing the horn his cheeks became considerably distended. In 1958 he was teaching his son, but using a reed, for the same reason that Wakame used a smaller horn.

Arupepe

The *Arupepe* from Teso country also in Elgon District, is constructed in very much the same way as the Bukhayo *Oluika*. It too is made from two horns joined together, reportedly bound by ox bladder. While the stouter section is again a cattle horn, the finer horn is that of the *Epoli*. One *Arupepe* seen was a little longer than the *Oluika* but otherwise of very much the same dimensions.

The method of playing this horn is unusual. There is no recognisable rhythm. There is the same breath control found with the Bukhayo *Oluika*, and the chief effect is that of long single notes on F below middle C, interspersed with musical flourishes including a high 'scooped' G, which may coincide with an intake of breath, as with the *Oluika*. The two main notes are the fundamental and another a major second above this. In one performance the first extended note lasted for some ten seconds, but later this was seldom more than four or five seconds. Very occasionally, there is also a pause on the G. The vocal part is spoken throughout and this was done by Longino Ebuu, the player of the *Adeudeu*, and a member of a Teso group of drummers. Here is a sketch of the general effect produced by the *Arupepe*.

The player, Lori, was teaching his son, but on a side-blown reed.

Conch Shell

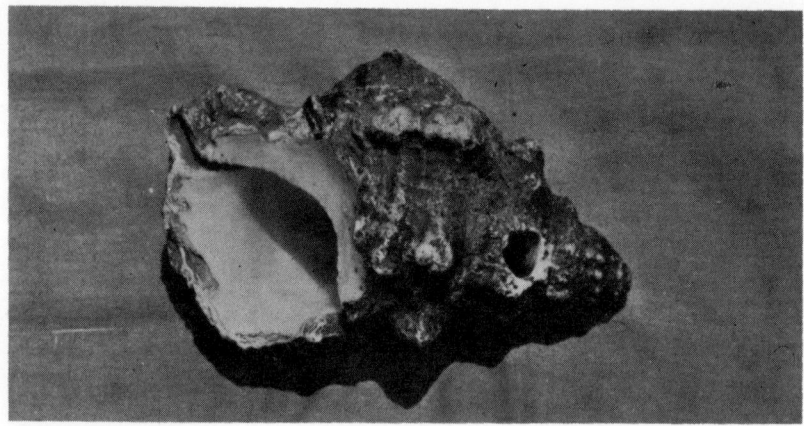

Conch Shell Horn (Giriama)

Another of nature's wind instruments is the conch shell picked up on the sea shore.

The one illustrated above, 20 cm (8 ins) long and 11.5 cm ($4\frac{1}{2}$ ins) across at its widest part, was acquired on a journey by road from Mombasa and Kilifi. A few miles north of Mombasa there is a creek, and although there is now a splendid bridge, formerly it was necessary to cross by ferry which was operated by a simple device by which men pulled on a chain fastened to each bank. This exercise was carried out literally, to a song and dance, to ensure that everyone pulled together, so conserving energy, and combining business with pleasure. The accompaniment was provided by the conch shell horn. The player produced different notes but the fundamental was E above middle C.

Fundamental

The shell had been in use for so long that some of the knobbles had worn quite smooth.

Mlele

Flutes of various kinds are very common in many parts of Africa. The variety which is found more often is that known as the fipple flute, which is rather like the recorder, an end-blown instrument. This type is also called the notched flute, because the player's breath is directed against a U or V shaped notch cut in the mouthpiece on the upper rim of the instrument as seen in the illustration below.

Isoka with *Mlele*

This is the *Mlele* from Tachoni country at the foot of Mount Elgon. It is made of bamboo. The one illustrated is nearly 47 cm (18½ ins) long. It has four holes and the tuning is most unusual, being made up of a series of semitones, the full range being a major third. The middle finger of the player's right hand is held firmly over the lowest hole the whole time. This is the tuning.

Here is a sketch of one song with the *Mlele* accompaniment.

Chivoti

The Wadigo on the coast of Kenya have a beautiful transverse flute which, unlike the fipple flute is held horizontally. This is a more highly developed instrument than the flute in Elgon district and is much less common. It is called *Chivoti* and is the only one of its kind found so far in Kenya. The instrument illustrated opposite is 26.5 cm (10½ ins) long and is made of bamboo. There are six holes but in any perform-

Sudi Mwakatsumi with *Chivoti* (Digo) and Salim Mbwana, with *Kayamba* (Digo)

ance watched, the one nearest the end was never covered. The end of the flute nearest the mouthpiece is closed.

The tuning raises problems. Played one after the other the notes sounded like this:

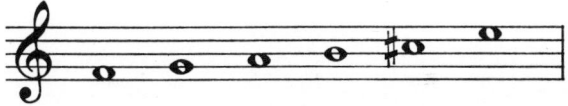

The notes deduced from hearing the instrument played are slightly different, as shown below, and even then there is some uncertainty as to whether the top note is an E or an F. If it were the latter, this would be very convenient as it would represent a simple pentatonic scale.

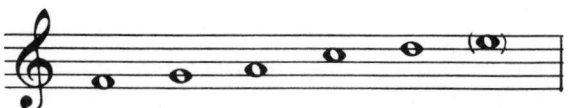

Within these acknowledged limits of precision, here is the transcription of a tune played on the *Chivoti*. For brevity certain repeated phrases have been omitted.

It has been seen that the role of instrumental music in Kenya is often regarded as simply that of providing an accompaniment to a song. The use of the *Chivoti* is not restricted in this way. Certainly there is a song, normally with some kind of percussion accompaniment, but the entry of the flute comes only when the song has finished, with the percussion continuing. There is a fuller transcription of this same piece of music with its percussion accompaniment on page 56.

Mwarutu

There is another little wind instrument in Digo country. It is the *Mwarutu*, a small ocarina made from the fruit of the *Mkwakwa* tree. It is rather like a small gourd and has three holes, one larger one in the middle to act as mouthpiece and two smaller ones stopped with the fingers. The four main notes of the instrument are as follows. There is some uncertainty about the B.

Bung'o or Nzumari

The most sophisticated wind instrument found in Kenya is the *Bung'o* or *Nzumari*, the former name given to it by the Waduruma and the other by the Wadigo. It is interesting to note that while the greatest variety of stringed instruments is to be found in Western Kenya, the most highly developed wind and percussion instruments are in the coastal region.

There are clear signs of Arabic influence in the *Nzumari*. The name itself recalls the Arabic instrument *Zummarah* and the decorations on the beautifully bell-shaped end reflect Arabic artistic traditions. One scholar, Karl Brambata, has said that this kind of instrument was known in the Egypt of the Pharaohs 2 700 years ago. This question of tracing the origin of African musical instruments to other parts of the world is sometimes overdone but in this case the indications of Arabic origin of the *Nzumari* seem fairly clear. Whatever its origins however, the important fact now is that it must be counted as one of Kenya's musical instruments.

The best way to describe the *Nzumari* is to examine it piece by piece. A double reed, such as that found in the oboe and which gives the instrument its distinctive timbre, is held in the mouth. This is made from the *Mvumo* reed grass. Next there is a shallow lip shield made from a section of fine coconut shell. This is followed by a 5 cm (2 ins) length of fine brass tubing which is fixed into the next section made of bamboo with a plug of cassava. It is in this 15 cm (6 ins) of bamboo that six holes are cut to produce the different notes. The bamboo is fastened in its turn to the bell-shaped carved wooden open end by a plaited ring of string.

The Nzumari is a powerful instrument and sounds very much like the chanter of the Scottish bagpipes in which there is also a double reed. Expert players display the same incredible breath control that was found with some of the horn players from Elgon and it is difficult to detect the places where breath is taken.

Two instruments studied revealed different systems of tuning, both of them pentatonic. One Duruma *Bung'o* was tuned as follows:

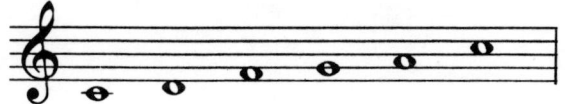

Bung'o or *Nzumari*

An *Nzumari* from Digo country was tuned like this:

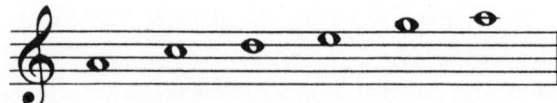

Three examples are given from a transcription of a performance on the Duruma *Bung'o*. First there is the arresting almost fanfare style opening, then the entry of the percussion accompaniment with the *Kayamba* and finally the firm rhythmic pattern of the *Bung'o* when accompanied by the Kayamba.

(i) The opening. Free and urgent

(ii) The entry of the Kayamba

In the extract shown below of the *Bung'o* and the *Kayamba*, there are two percussion effects which are explained on page 54. The theme on the *Bung'o* is only one of many heard in this performance.

Percussion Instruments

Early in 1970, the Post Office authorities issued a series of four stamps devoted to the musical instruments of East Africa. Those chosen were the *Adeudeu* and *Nzumari* from Kenya, the hand *Marimba* from Tanzania and the *Amadinda* xylophone from Uganda. There was no drum. Some members of the public raised the question as to why this was so. The omission was deliberate. Apparently everyone has heard of the African drum but many people both outside and inside Africa seem to know very little about any other African musical instrument. There is a general unawareness of the wealth of musical instruments of all kinds that are to be found all over Africa. The issue of stamps was therefore taken as an opportunity to educate the public on this matter.

There are of course all kinds of drums in Africa generally, and in Kenya in particular, played in any number of combinations with the most complicated contrasts in rhythm. It is interesting to notice that while words such as *ngoma* in Swahili describe drums in general, each individual drum has its own name.

Endonyi and Efumbu

There is a group of three drums played together in Bukusu country in Elgon and they consist of two identical metal based small drums called *Endonyi*, and one beautifully made long wooden drum known as *Efumbu*. The *Endonyi* are double ended but the *Efumbu* is open at the lower end. Originally the two *Endonyi* would also have had a wooden base but the use of tins in this case has already been referred to as one of those labour saving devices seen in the construction of instruments.

It would be quite impossible to discover the way in which the intricacies of the contrasting rhythms are built up, simply by listening to the drummers playing together, even 'live', let alone on a recording. The best method is to learn the part played by each drummer in turn, and to play that part with the others. In this way it can be found that

Tawayi and Ismael with two *Endonyi* Silali with *Efumbu*

so far as the *Endonyi* and the *Efumbu* are concerned there are really two rhythmic patterns, one of which is quite simple and the other more complex.

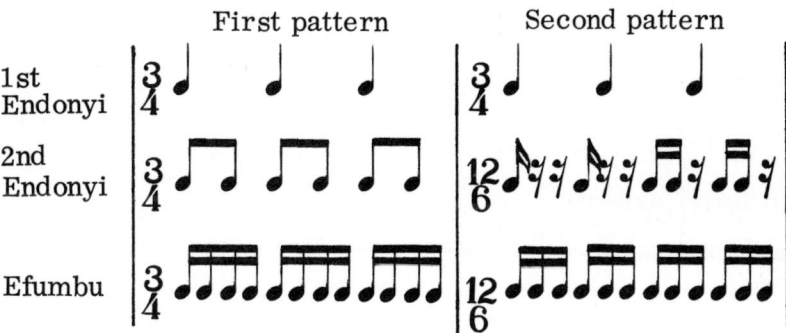

The first pattern is a simple one, being a straightforward subdivision of the main beat played by the first *Endonyi* into two and four by the second *Endonyi* and the *Efumbu*. To any African drummer this is exceedingly dull and so interesting variations are introduced.

The first *Endonyi* however continues with his regular simple crotchet beat throughout the performance and acts as a kind of rhythmic anchorage. In order to understand what is happening with the second *Endonyi* in the more complex pattern, it is best to look first at the *Efumbu* variations. Originally the *Efumbu* had twelve semi-quavers divided into three groups of four. Later these are divided into four groups of three. Exactly the same value for the semi-quaver is maintained throughout. The second *Endonyi* player bases his variations on those of the *Efumbu*, but only plays the first or the first two semi-quavers of each group of three. The variations of the second *Endonyi* are shown here as a regular pattern in half bars but in fact they are irregular, being governed by the whim of the drummer. It will be seen that in the second pattern, the second *Endonyi* and the *Efumbu* coincide only once with the first *Endonyi* on a strong beat, namely the first beat of the bar.

In conventional language what is happening in the variations is that the second *Endonyi* player and the *Efumbu* alternate between simple triple time and compound quadruple time against the constant simple triple time on the first *Endonyi*.

As shown here the impression is given that the drummers always start the different rhythms together. In practice there does not appear to be any particular system as to when each drummer changes his rhythm. It is quite possible to have the *Efumbu* playing his second pattern with the second *Endonyi* playing his first.

The two *Endonyi* are played with drum sticks each player using one only. The *Efumbu* is played simply with the hands.

Indonyi, Izidonyi and Ing'oma

There is a group of three drums very much like those from Bukusu country, which are found in the neighbouring district of Marach. One is the *Indonyi* and it is a small wooden barrel drum played with one stick. Another small cylindrical drum with a metal base is known as *Izidonyi*, and this is played with two sticks. Finally there is a long wooden barrel drum like the *Efumbu*, called *Ing'oma* which is played with both hands. The *Ing'oma* illustrated opposite was decorated with rather gaudy painted patterns.

Left – Thomas Akong'o with *Indonyi*; Centre – Omenya Oruiya with *Ing'oma*; Right – Makokha Owori with *Izidonyi*

Here is a transcription of a performance on these drums. It will be seen that the only one which displays any variety is the *Ing'oma*.

♩ = 132

Indonyi

Izidonyi

Ing'oma

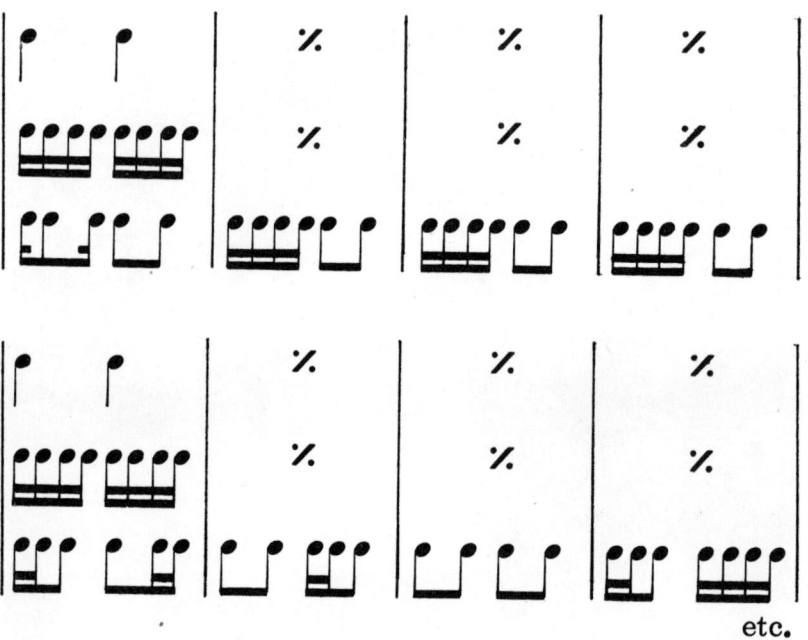

etc.

As with some of the stringed instruments, one of the players introduces the performance in plain speech, against the drumming, and there is a song by the same performer, again interspersed with spoken comment.

Atenesu

Another group of three drummers, from Teso district, use only two drums, called *Atenesu*, one of them being played on the top by one drummer and on the bottom by another. In this combination there is every possible variation in the use of hands or drum sticks. One player uses one hand and one stick, another two sticks, and the third both hands.

When the drums are heard separately there does not appear any particular complexity.

Square Atenesu

Round Atenesu – bottom

Round Atenesu – top

Longino Ebuu with square *Atenesu*, Martin Otuane playing on top of round *Atenesu* and Longino Omongoluko playing on bottom of round *Atenesu*

When these rhythms are combined it is at once clear that the player on the square *Atenesu* has a rhythm in compound quadruple time, while the others use a compound triple rhythm. Even when the players demonstrate their own part on their own, they maintain the same note values which are necessary for their first beat to coincide when playing together.

The player using the top of the round *Atenesu* wears ankle bells which coincide with his simple drum beat.

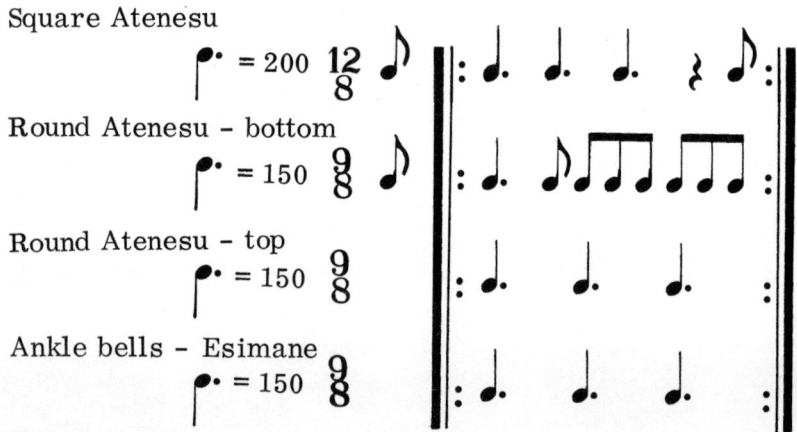

In this performance, there was a song in which many people joined as well as the drummers.

Mutiiti and Isuguti

In the Manyisi district of Mount Elgon there is a drum ensemble of three wooden cylindrical drums which taper towards the open end. They are each of a different size. The largest, called *Isuguti* is 71.5 cm (28½ ins) long with a drum head 20.5 cm (8 ins) in diameter. The narrow end of the drum is only 13 cm (5 ins) in diameter. The medium sized drum, also known as *Isuguti* is shorter and has a diameter of 15 cm (6 ins) at the drum head, tapering down to 12 cm (4¾ ins). The smallest of the three, the *Mutiiti* is only 44.5 cm long (17½ ins) with a diameter of 13.5 cm (5¼ ins) at the wider end tapering down to 10 cm (4 ins) at the other end. All three seen were made from the *Mukomare* tree.

The drums are hung over the shoulder, normally over the left shoulder so that the right hand can have free play. The drummer who was heard playing the *Mutiiti* was left handed, so he had to hang his drum over his right shoulder. None of the drummers used a drum stick, they all played with their hands.

Each of the drummers, Shioso with the big *Isuguti*, Mutoro with the smaller one, and Chimaisi with the *Mutiiti*, belonged to the third generation of drummers. Shioso and Chimaisi were already passing on their skills to their sons.

The leader of the trio would appear to be Chimaisi, as it is he who sings the song and also wears ankle bells on both legs.

In the following transcription some repeated bars have been omitted to show a greater variety of rhythmic patterns, the order of which seems quite spontaneous.

Mutiiti
=120
6/8
Isuguti (medium)
=120
2/4
Isuguti (large)
=120
2/4

Kayamba

The *Kayamba* is an important percussion instrument found chiefly at the coast although it is becoming popular up-country and is now frequently used elsewhere.

It is tray-shaped and of various sizes, the larger ones being some 41 cm (16 ins) long and 20.5 cm (8 ins) wide. It consists of two layers of reeds sewn together and secured to form a shallow compartment in which hard bright red and black seeds are contained. When the *Kayamba* is shaken to and fro as in the illustration on page 41, a rattle effect is produced.

With the best instruments a second percussion effect is produced. In the examples seen in the illustration on page 41 there is a strip of some part of the coconut palm fastened down the middle of the instrument and this is used as a clapper played with the thumbs.

The *Kayamba* is often used in contrasting rhythm with a song. A singer could accompany himself on the *Kayamba* in the following style.

Mchirima, Chapuo and Gandu

The most sophisticated drumming heard so far in Kenya is at the coast. The opportunity of studying styles in that area has been restricted to that of the Wadigo in Kwale district, but it is certain that similar skills are displayed by other groups living on the coastal belt.

The first important element to notice is that Digo drums are tuned to notes of a particular pitch, thus providing a melodic as well as a percussion accompaniment. With other drums in Kenya of indefinite pitch the required tension of the membrane is achieved by leaving drums in the sun, or holding them in front of a fire. This method is obviously quite inadequate with drums which have to be tuned to particular notes and the tuning is done in this case by tightening and loosening cords attached to a cane ring to which the membrane is

![drums photo]

Top left – *Bumbumbu*; Top centre – *Kayamba*; Top right – *Mchirima*; Centre – *Nzuga*; Left – *Chigandu*; Bottom right – *Gandu*

fastened. The illustration above shows clearly how this system works.

Some Digo drums are double-ended like the *Mchirima* in the top right corner of the photograph. This tapers slightly towards the bottom of the drum, but the *Chapuo*, not illustrated, which is another double-ended drum is regularly cylindrical being 38 cm (15 ins) long, and 20 cm (8 ins) in diameter for the whole length. The *Gandu* has legs, rather like a stool. All are wooden based. In one ensemble which included these drums, six performers took part.

Hamisi played four drums on his own, tuned like this.

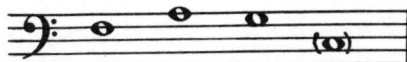

The uncertainty of the lowest note was removed in the performance, when it was clearly associated with a C in the flute part.

In the tuning of the double-ended *Chapuo*, played by Juma, there is a recurrence of the well-known interval of a perfect fourth.

It seems unlikely that the tuning of this drum to F♯–C♯ was intended to produce a deliberate clash with the F in the flute part and the other drums. In fact, the timbre of the drum neutralises the dissonance.

Masudi played the *Chivoti* flute, and Salim Mbwana, Sudi and Mohamed Bakari, all played the *Kayamba*.

Here is a transcription of part of the performance. The melodic contribution by the four drums is clear. They sound rather like a double bass played pizzicato. The occurrence of the middle C in this part raises difficulties as this is not one of the notes to which the drums were tuned. It may even be that this note comes from the *Chapuo*. It certainly occurs in bars 9 and 13 at a point where there is a middle C in the *Chapuo* part.

In the group of instrumentalists seen over, the sixty odd *Nzuga* ankle bells which Salim Mbwana is wearing can be seen more clearly in the photograph on page 55. It is difficult to see Mohamed Bakari's fifth drum as it is held between his knees. The drum on the extreme left is the *Bumbumbu*. The large tapering drum is the *Mchirima*, and the smaller cylindrical one is the *Chapuo*. That on the right is the *Chigandu*. The five drums are tuned like this.

The strikers used with the small brass gong – *Ukaya*, bottom right, are made of plaited grass – *Mlala*, which is an imaginative way of producing a pleasant tone. The rhythm of the *Nzuga* and *Ukaya* is this:

Left – Salim Mbwana with *Nzuga*, Juma Masafari with *Nzumari*;
Centre – Mohamed Bakari with five drums; Bottom right – Mwinyi with *Ukaya*
(See overleaf.)

What of the Future?

These *Notes* show clearly that traditional musical instruments in Kenya flourish now, but the question which has to be asked is whether there is any future for them, and the skilled musicians who play them. There are certainly three factors which may affect the perpetuation of instrumental music in Kenya. There is the material reward the musicians should enjoy, the recognition of their skills, and the pattern of life to which their music-making belongs.

The question of economics may very well not have occurred to traditional instrumentalists – as yet, although they are already justifiably concerned about the use to which recordings of their performances are put. Generally speaking however they have been playing their instruments all these years because they belong to a musical family, and also because they obviously gain real satisfaction and enjoyment from doing so. Many of them have spent so much time acquiring their skills, that they have never bothered to embark on any other training and so would find it difficult to obtain any other kind of employment. So they take what they are given for their services and do not question their financial position. On the other hand, this kind of situation is unlikely to tempt those who might have followed in their footsteps, to take the trouble to undergo the discipline required to learn to play these instruments. The Dance Band is often a more attractive proposition, where some facility with the guitar will demand much less skill and command much greater material reward.

With regard to the second point, it is important that traditional instrumentalists should be recognised in society as embodying an important part of the cultural heritage, and belonging to the category of professionals. This is not always so, but there are hopeful signs of a new outlook. The syllabus for music in the East Africa Certificate of Education now includes a proper proportion of African music, and this includes performance on a traditional instrument. Within this academic context, there will surely emerge a growing respect for these instruments and the men that play them. The young people who will have to learn how to play such instruments at school, will do so within the framework of their general musical studies and it is to be hoped that they will recognise not only their present worth, but also possibilities for future development.

The third factor which may affect the future of traditional instruments is the pattern of life to which their music belongs. Few will probably dispute the fact that on the whole, African instrumentalists are at home in the old way of life. They seem to have got left behind in the main stream of revolutionary social change. Surely every attempt should be made to encourage these musicians to adapt themselves to the changing, or changed situation and find contemporary patterns of life in which they can still carry on their most musical of careers. Otherwise there is a grave danger that when the older ways are forsaken, they may disappear too.

Appendix

Classification of Instruments – Hornbostel–Sachs

Idiophones
Instruments made of naturally sonorous materials not needing any additional tension.
Chisasi – Bukusu, rattle
Esidiri – Marach, toe ring
Esimane – Teso, ankle bells
Ibiturani – Kuria, bells
Ikengere – Bukusu, metal
Kayamba – Coastal areas, Reed rattle
Luhengere – Bukusu, wooden 'arch'
Mbiirii – Tende, Finger bells
Nzuga – Coastal areas, ankle bells
Tendeche – Marach, ankle bells
Ukaya – Digo, gong

Aerophones
Wind instruments.
Arupepe – Teso, horn, side blown
Bung'o – Duruma, double reed wind instrument, end blown
Chivoti – Digo, flute, side blown
Conch shell – Giriama, side blown
Mlele – Tachoni, flute, end blown
Mwarutu – Digo, ocarina
Nzumari – Digo, double reed instrument, end blown
Oluika – Bukhayo, horn, side blown
Oluika – Tachoni, horn, side blown

Membranophones
The sound is produced by a membrane stretched over an opening.
Atenesu – Teso, metal based drum
Chapuo – Digo, cylindrical drum, wooden based
Efumbu – Bukusu, barrel drum, wooden based
Endonyi – Bukusu, cylindrical drum, metal based
Gandu – Digo, drum, wooden based
Indonyi – Marach, barrel drum, wooden based
Ing'oma – Marach, barrel drum, wooden based
Isuguti – Manyisi, drum, wooden based
Izidonyi – Marach, cylindrical drum, metal based
Mchirima – Digo, conical drum, wooden based
Mutiiti – Manyisi, drum, wooden based

Chordophones
Chordophones are instruments with strings.
Adeudeu – Teso, arched harp
Ntono – Tende, Stick-zither
Litungu – Bukusu, bowl lyre
Litungu – Kuria, bowl lyre
Obokano – Kisii, bowl lyre
Obukhana – Marach, bowl lyre
Orutu – Luo, bowed lute
Siiriri – Bukusu, bowed lute
Wandindi – Kikuyu, bowed lute

Information concerning the classification of musical instruments by Hornbostel and Sachs is taken from 'The History of Musical Instruments' Sachs, Curt, first published U.S.A. 1940 and in U.K. 1942.